THE GULF OF NAPLES

A wonderful journey through art, history
and natural beauties to discover the pearls
of the Gulf and the archaeological sites.

CONTENTS

THE ISLANDS OF THE GULF

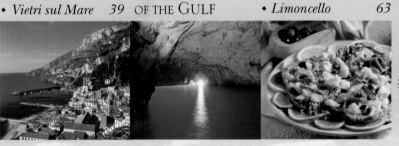

THE AMALFI COAST

THE TYPICAL NEAPOLITAN CUISINE

Naples

Looking on to the gulf of the same name, the city enjoys one of the most fascinating views in Europe: the beauty of nature is associated with the mild climate and the clear sky and colour of the sea illuminate important architectural masterpieces.

Forgetting about the car and walking is the best way to discov-

Villa Comunale.

er the thousand colours of Naples, unravelling the fascinating tangle of its ancient centre, with a sur-

The Gulf of Naples with the Vesuvius in the background.

The impressive mass of the Maschio Angioino.

prise at every corner thanks to the views of the sea, setting your pace to the very special one of a city that really seems, beyond all clichés, to

The Cathedral of San Gennaro.

Umberto I Gallery.

invent life every moment of the day. On the hill of Vomero there are examples of Neapolitan baroque to be found, the gardens of the Certosa and the fort built by the Angevin sovereigns. Looking towards the seafront and the maritime station, you can see the impressive mass of the Maschio Angioino fort and, nearby, the massive sil-

The Immacolatella Fountain.

Castel dell'Ovo.

houette of the Castel dell'Ovo. A funicular railway leads to the

heart of the city, the area called Spaccanapoli, of ancient Greco-Roman origin, with the Church of Jesus (Chiesa del Gesù) the Monastery of Santa Chiara, the Monte di Pietà and the Filomarino and Marigliano palaces. Via Toledo, the most famous promenade, leads to the Umberto I Gallery, the San Carlo Theatre and the splendid Piazza del Plebiscito. From Forcella you reach Piazza delle Mura Greche and, after crossing Corso Umberto, the ancient Porta Nolana.

Piazza Plebiscito, the Royal Palace.

THE *VESUVIUS*

This symbol of Naples famous all over the world is considered by experts as one of the five most dangerous volcanoes in the world. But it is also one of the most spectacular. From the mouth of its crater, the whole of the Gulf of Naples is dominated, the plain of the river Sarno and the plain between Naples and Caserta.

Over 800 metres, the large cone of the volcano is divided into an impressive natural amphitheatre formed by the remains of the

The inside of the crater seen from above.

crater of mount Somma – which touches 1132 metres with the Punta del Nasone – at the centre of which there rises the highest peak, the Great Cone, 1281 metres high. Outstanding varieties of peaches, cherries and apricots and vineyards, from which a wine of a special quality is obtained, grow on its fertile slopes.

POMPEII

It owes its fame to the sad end that buried it in 79 AD, following the eruption of Vesuvius, together with Herculaneum and Stabia.

Ashes rained down on the ancient Roman city, burying it under a 7 metre-thick layer in only 30 hours. Many of its 30,000 inhabitants died, but Pompeii paradoxically remained intact for over 1500 years, until the first chance discoveries in the 16th century.

It was not until 1748, thanks to the

The remains of the Temple of Jupiter.

Bourbon government of Naples, that a systematic campaign of excavations was started which led, in 1763, to identifying the position of the city with certainty, thanks to the discovery of an inscription.

Since then, the archaeological excavations have continued until the present, with numerous campaigns that have become increasingly scientific and accurate. Today, more or less three-fifths of the inhabited centre, which covered about 66 hectares, have been

Garden of the fugitives.

brought to light.

The extraordinary state of preservation of the objects found, precious evidence of daily life (from freshly baked bread to the graffiti on the walls, to the paintings that acted as election posters), of homes, buildings, temples and baths, as well as the remains of some two thousand victims (fleeing men and women, children, gladiators and dogs), make Pompeii a unique case in the world for the study of Roman architecture and Latin society in the 1st century AD.

Many finds and some of the finest frescoes and mosaic floors are currently on display at

The Faunus.

The bronze statue of Apollo near the portico of the sacred area.

House of the Vettii: goldsmith cupids.

the Archaeological Museum of Naples. In 1997, the archaeological area was declared patrimony of humanity by UNESCO.

There are two entrances to the area of the excavations, one near the Porta Marina, not far from the exit on the Naples-Reggio Calabria motorway and the other near the Amphitheatre, closer to the present-day town.

There are many possible itineraries

Amphiteather built in 80 B.C.

(even if not all the dwellings that have been unearthed can be visited) and all the main places of life at the time can be admired, from the Forum to the Theatre, from the Baths to the Barracks of the Gladiators to the countless temples. The frescoes present in many rich dwellings and almost entirely salvaged are splendid.

The portico in front of the shops of the Macellum.

Herculaneum

Destroyed in 79 AD by the eruption of Vesuvius, it was discovered by chance in 1709 when a peasant, digging a well, found ancient marbles that he then sold.

The commander of an Austrian contingent stationed in the area, after having seen them, started the excavations, which in the subsequent archaeological campaigns, brought to light more than a city, as in the case of Pompeii, but an infinite series of precious finds, statues and buried jewellery. Since 1927 some important public buildings – the baths, the gymnasium, the theatre – and various private homes have also been unearthed.

Near the city stood the vast and luxurious Villa of the Papyruses, which belonged to a rich and cultivated aristocrat: the hundreds of rolls of papyrus found, containing Greek philosophical texts, and the tens of bronze and marble statues are of enormous historic and documentary interest.

A view of the town with the Vesuvius in the background.

PAESTUM

An ancient centre of Magna Greece, it owes its present-day name to the Romans who, in 273 BC, established a colony there. In the imperial period, Paestum began a long and progressive decadence, until it was abandoned for good in the 8th century, due to the area turning into a swamp and the gradual spread of malaria. The city was only partially brought to the light by archaeological excavations and shows the typical Roman layout with impressive walls, the Temple of Ceres in the

Temple of Neptune, the façade facing south.

Temple of Ceres.

north and, in the centre, the public area, with the forum, the comitia (for meetings of the

The tomb of the Diver.

assembly) and the Capitolium.

Behind the forum there stood the amphitheatre and a Hellenistic gymnasium with a large pool.

To the south there was the large urban sanctuary of Hera, known to all as the Basilica.

Alongside it stands the splendid Temple of Neptune, a canonical example of the Doric style.

The whole complex is of exceptional beauty, also thanks to the excellent state of preservation of the buildings. The whole archaeological area of the city has been included by UNESCO in the list of sites to be protected as the patrimony of humanity.

Near the city, at the mouth of the Sele, the ruins of the Greek sanctuary of Hera (Heraion) can be admired. The National Archaeological Museum of Paestum, founded in 1952, is near the ancient city.

THE SORRENTO PENINSULA

Its southern side is universally known as the Amalfi coast.

But the northern side is also rich in charm, extending like a finger towards Capri. Its westernmost tip, Punta Campanella, is the last offshoot of the slope towards the sea of the Lattari Mountains and you can follow an itinerary that has been made famous by the poets and artists who have loved it and celebrated it.

The starting point is Castellammare di Stabia, famous for the excavations of the Roman villas of the ancient Stabiae, which was also buried by the eruption of Vesuvius in 79 AD. From here, it is worth going up Mount Faito, from where there is a splendid view overlooking the whole of the Peninsula.

To avoid the ascent, there is a cable-car which leaves from the centre of Castellammare, near the station of the Circumvesuviana.

By car, on the other hand, it is possible to continue the itinerary through Vico Equense to Sorrento. It is only a distance of twenty kilometres, but with very beautiful natural scenery and landscape, framed by the splendid greenery of olive trees and orange trees and interspersed with panoramic spots which offer unforgettable views of the Gulf of Naples.

SORRENTO

From a tuff terrace overhanging the sea, it dominates the Peninsula of the same name that looks on to the Gulf of Naples.

Probably of Greek origin, in Roman times it took the name of Surrentum, becoming a privileged holiday resort for the Roman aris-

The enchanting coast of the Gulf of Sorrento.

tocracy. The orthogonal design of the streets of the old city centre still reveals the Roman origins of Sorrento which towards the mountain is protected by sixteenth-century walls.

Of note are the 15th century Cathedral (Duomo), with its neo-Gothic façade, and the Church of St. Francis of Assisi, with the small fourteenth-century cloister.

The Correale Museum has a dis-

A characteristic foreshortening with the façade of the Cathedral.

The fourteenth century Cloister of the Church of St. Francis of Assisi.

play of Greek and Roman remains and Capodimonte porcelain.

The most classic walk is the one that winds through the historic centre of the town, through Piazza Tasso, Via Tasso and Via San Cesareo. Not far from Sorrento, these are reached by going

Piazza Tasso.

Monument to Sant'Antonino Abate.

down from Capo di Sorrento and passing through the ruins of the ancient Roman villa of Pollio Felice. The Bagni della Regina

The Bagni della Regina Giovanna.

Giovanna are a splendid natural swimming-pool, surrounded by sheer rocky walls. This great beauty spot is definitely worth a visit.

Marina Grande.

Massa Lubrense

It stands on a green and undulating plain over the sea.
Bathing is possible at nearby Marina della Lobra, or at the more distant Marina del Cantone, the largest beach of the Peninsula.

Sant'Agata sui Due Golfi

It dominates the two gulfs of Naples and Salerno, from where excellent and sunny views can be enjoyed. It is a holiday resort, standing at an altitude of almost 400 m. From the nearby Monastery of the Desert moments of peace can be relished observing the panorama from the splendid terrace.

Vico Equense

This is a pleasant seaside resort, with fine beaches that stretch under a balcony of tuff on which the town is built. The ancient fourteenth-century Cathedral is very beautiful.
A panoramic excursion also includes a visit to the nearby Seiano and Punta Scutolo, from where the Gulf of Naples and the Piana di Sorrento can be seen.

THE *A*MALFI *C*OST

*T*his geographical area of the Campania region is identified with the southern side of the Peninsula of Sorrento.

Amalfi.

The Lattari mountains, which offer their protection making the climate particularly mild, slope down to the Tyrrhenian Sea, enriching the splendid landscapes with lush and typically Mediterranean vegetation.
You should take the road all the way from Sant'Agata on the Two Gulfs to Vietri sul Mare, with scenery that is both wild and gentle.
The main centres are all where deep valleys meet the sea and the rounded and soft lines of the coast contrast with the sharp angles of the mountain.
A world-famous area of tourism, the Coast owes its name to its main centre, Amalfi, which stands at the mid-point of the coast.
Amalfi was the oldest of the four Italian Marine Republics and in medieval times extended its supremacy to the neighbouring towns.
Since 1997, the Amalfi Coast has been part of UNESCO's patrimony of humanity.

Positano.

AMALFI

A town in the province of Salerno, tradition has it that the Romans founded it in the 4th century AD and as the seat of the bishop it was subject from the 6th century to the Eastern Roman Empire and to the Longobards. Independent from the 9th century, it became established as a marine republic and power in the next two centuries. Sacked by its

A panoramic view of the city of Amalfi. Above: The Grotta dello Smeraldo (Emerald Grot

rival Pisa, in 1135, it flourished anew under the Swabians, becoming in the subsequent centuries the feud of various families of nobles (Colonna, Orsini, Sanseverino, Piccolomini). The "Tavola Amalfitana", kept in the Civic Museum, shows the famous maritime laws used in the Mediterranean until the 16th century. The seafront is the classic walk and one of the most beautiful along the whole coast. The sixteenth-century Tower, the Arsenal and the Albergo dei Cappuccini, which occupies a thirteenth-century convent, stand out. Characterised by white houses built on the slope, it has a Cathedral (Duomo) and a small Museum of Paper. Its main resource is tourism, favoured all year round by the mild climate and the spectacular beauty of the surroundings.

The beautiful façade of the Cathedral with its imposing flight of steps.

POSITANO

Amongst the most popular resorts of the Coast, Positano rivalled in the past with Amalfi for the military supremacy on this strait and today it still competes with it for popularity with tourists.

The inhabited part descends from the slopes of Mount Sant'Angelo to Tre Pizzi (1444 m, the highest summit of the Lattari Mountains), nestling on the hillside with the characteristic streets with steps and arched roofs of the houses. The very old fishermen's homes are the finest architectural sight in the village: they are cube-

Panorama of the Belvedere.

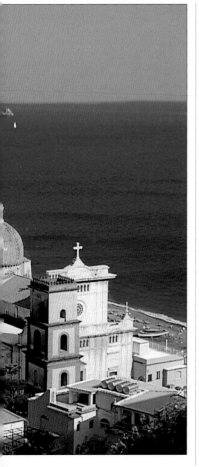

shaped, with few windows and are covered by a semi-spherical dome. With their almost dazzling whiteness, they stand out against the thick vegetation that surrounds the village.

Going up to the Belvedere you can enjoy the view of the whole village, huddled around the Parish Church of Santa Maria Assunta, with the background of the sea and the colourful eighteenth-century majolica dome.

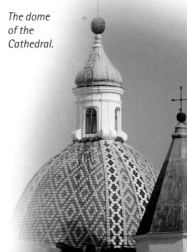

The dome of the Cathedral.

ATRANI

Just 1 km. from Amalfi, Atrani is a small and picturesque village, set between the sea and the rocky faces of the Lattari Mountains.

The Doges of Amalfi were elected here, in the church of San Salvatore de Bireto, which can still be visited. Characteristic are the ceramics produced here, with noble and ancient traditions.

A characheristic view of Atrani.

MINORI

A charming place, where the blue of the sea blurs with the green of the vineyards and the citrus groves wrenched from the mountain thanks to the system of terrace cultivation. When Amalfi was at the peak of its splendours, it was an important arsenal.

Very evocative are the remains of the ancient Roman villa, of which important parts are preserved together with a collection of objects coming from other excavations, including undersea finds.

MAIORI

This is one of the most delightful spots of the Amalfi Coast. The fine sandy beach contrasts with the bright colours of the village, from which the strong colours of the dome, intricately covered with majolica tiles, of the famous church of Santa Maria al Mare stand out. The village spreads out like horseshoe around the sea.

There is a marvellous view from the terraces covered with lemon trees. In the surroundings, the ancient Abbey of Santa Maria de Olearia and Capo d'Orso, another panoramic spot, can be visited.

RAVELLO

Higher than the so-called Valley of the Dragon, it offers sumptuous and famous dwellings, with gar-

A panoramic view of Ravello.

dens of incomparable beauty, including Villa Rufolo, whose fragrant garden inspired Richard Wagner to compose the music of Parsifal. Just as beautiful is Villa Cimbrone, and from its Belvedere there is an exceptional view of the sea. But Ravello is not only famous for these two splendid buildings. The village, one of the most popular along the Amalfi Coast, has kept its ancient charm intact, made even more exotic by the Moorish-style and Sicilian - inspired architecture of its villas and simpler houses and gardens. Many have kept small porches which frame the doors.

The "Camo" Coral Museum is also to be visited, alongside the Duomo and the villas mentioned. In the surrounding area, an excursion to the village of Scala is worthwhile, with its fine medieval cathedral restructured in the eighteenth century.

VIETRI SUL MARE

It has linked its name with ceramics, which shine on the dome of the Parish Church of San Giovanni Battista, enriched with polychrome majolica, and which fill the many crafts shops of the village.

The seaside resorts of Marina di Vietri and Cetara are nearby, whilst a visit must also be made to Raito, standing above the sea, which has a museum of ceramics and from where there is a beautiful view of the whole of Vietri.

ISLE OF CAPRI

The Faraglioni seen from the Mount Solaro.

CAPRI

The island of Capri is reached from the Port of Sorrento, with ferries leaving frequently to link it with the mainland. The landing place is Marina Grande, from where it is possible to take the funicular railway to arrive at the

The Piazzetta.

centre, perched at 142 metres above sea level on a natural terrace, from where you can reach Piazza Umberto Primo, the famous Piazzetta. It is the "lounge" of Capri, one of the most elegant and famous in the world. Its renown began in the 1950s and has never ceased: it is not difficult to meet famous people here, of the many who have a home on Capri.

In the many films made on the

Marina Grande, the Harbour.

island, the Piazzetta has always been the central point of the scenes and the actors wind down after shooting. The custom for tourists is to sip a coffee at the tables of the bar in perfect peace and quiet and from there watch Marina Grande below, the island's main port, and the panorama going out to sea. From here you can continue through the streets, until reaching the Certosa di San Giacomo.

Around the Certosa there are various panoramic points of view, but which can be reached only by returning towards the town and taking narrow paths, often with steps. The most beautiful views are enjoyed from the Belvedere

Cannone and from the Belvedere di Tragara. From here you can continue to the Faraglioni with a short walk of about twenty minutes.

The Faraglioni, the most famous attraction of Capri known all over the world, owe their name to a particular geological formation, of calcareous origin, consisting of high cliffs, shaped by the wind and the sea, which rise up in isolation near the coast.

With a short walk from the centre of Capri you can reach a panoramic spot from where there is the best view of these monuments made of rock.

Still on foot, in about thirty minutes, you can reach, by taking a small road eastwards, the Natural Arch and the Matermania Grotto, two natural formations of great beauty.

From here, you can make a circle, going back to Capri from the

The Natural Arch.

Belvedere di Tragara. Again eastwards, compared to the town of Capri, you can reach, in about 45 minutes' walk, Villa Jovis, the ancient home of the Emperor Tiberius, standing on a rocky precipice from where there is a fantastic view over the Gulf of Salerno and the Gulf of Naples.

Those who wish to complete the visit of the island, can reach Anacapri, the other town on the small island (just 11 square kilometres) from Capri. Higher than Capri, it is also an elegant village.

Panorama of Marina Grande seen from Anacapri.

Villa Jovis.

From the centre you can take the chairlift (from Piazza della Vittoria) to Monte Solaro, and from its 589 metres you can dominate the whole of the island.
Again from the centre, a long walk, all flat, takes you to the Belvedere della Migliara. Lastly, leaving from Anacapri, you can go north-west by a little road that passes by the Roman Villa and then contin- ues for another 2 kilometres to the Torre di Damecuta, an ancient

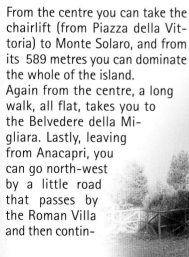

Torre di Damecuta.

watchtower built in the 12th century. The Grotta Azzurra, the most famous of Capri's sea grot- tos, is an ancient cavity of karstic origin rediscovered in 1826 by the German painter August Ko-

The Blue Grotto.

pisch. The breathtaking blue of the sea in the grotto, hence its name, is due to the fact that the daylight penetrates by refraction through a wide opening under the sea.

ISLE OF ISCHIA

The largest of the Flegrean Islands and the largest in the Gulf of Naples, it lies 7 nautical miles from the coast. Of volcanic origin (the most recent eruption was in 1302), its coasts are indented with, between capes and promontories, a few but splendid bays

Sant'Angelo.

Forio.

opening up, from where the famous sunsets can be admired, accompanied, for the luckiest, by the fleeting apparition of the "green ray" , the fine blade of light on the horizon that has the power to make love last eternally.
From the sanctuary of Santa Maria del Soccorso, in Forio, it is even possible to catch a glimpse of Fata Morgana, a mirage due to a particular contrast of refractions that makes distant land seem close, like the

Pontine islands. The mountainous landscape conceals in the interior, amongst pines and chestnuts, the renowned citrus groves and vines. The main centre of the

*Sanctuary
of Santa Maria
del Soccorso.*

island is divided between Ischia Ponte (the fishing village with the islet of Castello connected by the Aragonese bridge) and Ischia

The Aragonese Castle.

Porto, with the pine forest and the beaches. The Church of Santa Restituta, the protector of Ischia, should be visited. The island is also

popular for its spa of volcanic origin; in fact it is rich in thermal waters (saline-bromide-iodic, bicarbonate alkaline and slightly radioactive), which offer beneficial treatments all year round in a setting of unique

beauty. The most important are the Terme Comunali di Ischia, inaugurated in 1845, which are near the port.

But there are also thermal baths in Casamicciola, a centre which in 1883 was destroyed by a terrible earthquake, and in Lacco Ameno, characteristic for the mushroom-

Cartaromana Beach.

shaped rock that rises up nearby on the sea and its popular beach.

Casamicciola.

Lacco Ameno with its characteristic "Fungo", a mushroom-shaped rock.

THE *T*YPICAL NEAPOLITAN CUISINE

The Italian gastronomic products best known the world over originate from here. We are talking about pizza and spaghetti. But the traditional imagination also has had free rein to marvellous effect in the preparation of confectionery and ice creams, cheese and milk products. without forgetting wines and liqueurs. The most typical confectionery products include: zeppole, babà, pastiera, struffoli, sfogliatelle, cassatine, mostaccioli, roccocò, delizie al limone, casatiello and sanguinaccio. A mention of honour must be given obviously to coffee, a genuine urban ritual for all self-respecting Neapolitans.

Margherita Pizza

Roll out the dough and place it in an oven tray. Pour the olive oil on the pastry and spread with the tomatoes.

Cover with sliced mozzarella and generously season with salt and a sprinkle of pepper.

Place the baking tray on the middle shelf in a preheated oven at 200°C and leave to cook for 20 minutes. Serve the pizza piping hot, garnish with the fresh basil and pour over a dash of olive oil.

Ingredients for 4 people:

- 400 g pizza dough
- 300 g buffalo mozzarella or fior di latte cheese
- 400 g chopped, tinned tomatoes
- extra-virgin olive oil
- 2 sprigs fresh basil
- salt and pepper

Spaghetti with Clams

Wash the clams well under running water and then put them in a pan where one glass of oil has been heated with the garlic. When the clams open up, remove them from the pan and extract the clams from the shells, filtering the remaining liquid through a piece of linen to eliminate any sand.

Whilst you cook the spaghetti, put the clams back in the pan with the filtered liquid, 4 spoons of oil and warm up.

Adjust to taste with pepper and at the end add the spaghetti and chopped parsley. Mix the spaghetti in the pan with the clams and serve straight from the pan.

Ingredients for 4 people:

- *400 g spaghetti*
- *1 kg clams*
- *2 cloves of garlic*
- *1 small bunch of parsley*
- *olive oil*
- *pepper and salt*

VESUVIAN TORTIGLIONI

Cut the plum tomatoes in half length wise and place them in a frying pan with their juice, oil, wine and the slightly crushed garlic (making sure you have removed the core), oregano, and salt and pepper.

Cover and cook on a moderate heat for twenty minutes stirring from time to time with a wooden spoon. Dice the mozzarella cheese and leave to drain in a colander. Boil the tortiglioni in plenty of salted water. When the pasta is firm to the touch, drain and add to the pan with the tomatoes. Remove the garlic and cook on a low heat so the pasta absorbs the sauce well. Add the mozzarella and stir evenly into the pasta. Transfer the pasta on to a hot pasta bowl. Serve this succulent first course immediately.

Ingredients for 4 people:

- *400 g tortiglioni pasta*
- *500g tinned plum tomatoes*
- *1 dl extra virgin olive oil*
- *2 garlic cloves*
- *1/2 glass dry white wine*
- *1 teaspoon oregano*
- *250 g mozzarella cheese*
- *salt and pepper*

NEAPOLITAN MINESTRONE

Roast the pepper in the oven, remove the charred skin and cut it into pieces. Wash and roughly chop all the vegetables, finely chop the parsley, basil, cabbage and chicory. Put everything into a pan with two and a half litres of water, and bring to a boil. Separately brown the pancetta with the garlic and then add them with the oil to the vegetables. Cook on a low heat with the lid on. When it is nearly cooked, season with salt and pepper, and

Ingredients for 4 people:

- 50 g pancetta
- 2 cloves of garlic
- 1 carrot
- 1 onion
- 1 stalks of celery
- 1 handful of parsley
- 1 tomato
- 1 aubergine
- 2 potatoes
- 100 g beans (shelled)
- 1 courgette
- 1 small piece of cabbage
- 1 bunch of chicory
- 1 yellow bell pepper
- 1 bunch of basil
- grated Parmesan cheese
- oil
- salt and pepper

add the grated Parmesan. Mix, switch the heat off and leave with the lid on for about ten minutes. Serve warm, each person adding oil to taste. The presence of the pepper and aubergine in this minestrone gives a slightly spicy flavour.

FISH CAPONATA

Remove the skin and bones from the boiled fish. Break up the fish with a fork and garnish with salt, pepper, 4 tablespoons of oil and the lemon juice. Dissolve the sugar in a little vinegar in a soup bowl and dip the frisella in the vinegar, one by one, until they are soft. Place the frisella on individual plates and spoon over the fish. Remove any tough stalks from the two salads, then wash, dry and cut the salad into very thin strips. Garnish with a little oil, salt and pepper and place on top of the fish. Drain the anchovy fillets, remove the stones from the olives and chop them into small pieces, cut the peppers into strips and arrange on top of the frisella with the capers.
Wash and dry the orange and lemon, cut into thin slices, removing the seeds with the point of a knife, and arrange them around the frisella. Ideal for those who love unusual and appetising fish dishes.

Ingredients for 4 people:

- *4 Frisella*
- *1 boiled sea fish (700 g)*
- *extra virgin olive oil*
- *vinegar*
- *sugar*
- *lemon juice*
- *1 lettuce head - spiky lettuce head*
- *4 anchovy fillets in oil capers*
- *4 pickled peppers in vinegar*
- *4 black and 4 green olives*
- *1 orange - lemon*
- *salt and pepper*

FISHERMAN STYLE SEABASS

Scale the fish, discard the entrails, wash carefully and dry.

In a bowl prepare a marinade with oil, finely chopped garlic and parsley, the juice of two lemons, salt and pepper.

Pour this mixture onto the basses and then dispose them on a hot grill. Cook them for about 3 minutes on each side and serve immediately.

Ingredients for 4 people:

- *2 seabasses, 800 g each*
- *1 dl extra-virgin olive oil*
- *3 cloves of garlic*
- *1 handful of parsley*
- *2 lemons*
- *salt and pepper*

PEPERONATA

Wash, trim and deseed the peppers and remove any white pith and cut into thin strips. Heat the oil in a large saucepan, preferably an earthenware pot, and fry the finely chopped

onion, chilli pepper, and the pounded garlic (it must be removed afterwards), but do not allow it to brown. Add the peppers, the chopped tomatoes and season with the salt and pepper. Stir well, making sure the peppers do not stick to the bottom of the pan, and cook on a medium heat, then a low heat for approximately one hour until the vegetables are cooked through and well combined. This dish can be served both hot and cold. You can also add black olives and pieces of red chilli pepper to make this dish even more appetising.

Ingredients for 4 people:

- *1,5 kg fresh peppers*
- *2 onions - cloves of garlic*
- *6 juicy plum tomatoes*
- *2 tablespoons olive oil*
- *black olives*
- *1 red chilli pepper*
- *salt and pepper*

Neapolitan Pastiera

Pastry: Mix the flour and sugar and make a well with the flour. Add the chopped butter and the egg yolks. Knead well and leave to one side. Meanwhile, prepare the filling by pouring the cracked wheat, milk, butter and lemon rind into a saucepan and cook for 10 minutes, stirring occasionally. Spread out the ricotta cheese in a bowl with a fork and add the 4 egg yolks and 1 egg white, the wheat, candied fruit, chopped into small pieces, and the orange flower water. Prepare the cream with the ingredients listed above and add it to the filling. Roll out the pastry, making sure it is not too thin, and place into a greased and floured cake tray.

Fill with the filling and even out with a spatula. Make strips out of the remaining pastry cut-offs and lay them over the cake to form a lattice design. Place in the oven at a temperature of 180°C and this masterpiece of Neapolitan cuisine will be ready in an hour and a half.

Ingredients for 4 people:

pastry:	cream:
• 500 g flour	• 250 g sugar
• 250 g butter	• 1/2 litre milk
• 250 g sugar	• 5 eggs
• 3 eggs	

filling:

• 500 g ricotta cheese	• 2 tablespoons
• 250 g sugar	• orange flower
• 150 g candied fruit	water
• g butter	• 400 g cooked
4 eggs	cracked wheat

Limoncello

Select fresh lemons and wipe with a damp cloth. Peel them, taking care to cut only the yellow part of the rind and remove the white one. Place the yellow rind into a large glass jar with the alcohol and allow to stand for 10 days. This period elapsed, boil the water with the sugar for 5 minutes; allow the syrup to cool and add it to the jar together with the lemon peel infusion. One week later, filter the liquid and put it into a bottle. It is an excellent digestive to drink cheerfully with friends!

Ingredients:

- 6 lemons
- 1 litre of 95° Alcohol
- 1 litre of water
- 700 g of sugar

Editorial conception:
Casa Editrice RotalSele srl
Via Cascina Belcasule, 8
20141 Milano - Italia
e-mail: rotalsele@rotalsele.com

Distributed by:
EUROVIMAR S.R.L.
Via Nolana, 379
80045 Pompei (NA)
Tel. 081.850.49.77
Telefax 081.856.13.51
e-mail: eurovimar@eurovimar.it

Publishing Editor:
Ermanno Stucchi

Editing:
Daniela Santori

64

Text:
Riccardo Oldani

Graphic design and makeup:
Alberto Grazioli
Alessio Buono

Project and iconographic research:
Salvatore Scalogna

Photographs:
The photographs belong the the Photographic Archives
of the Casa Editrice Rotalsele.

Property of Cartography:
RotalSele srl - Milano

Printed in UE
by RotalSele srl - Milano